my thoughts your journal our book

by
Abe Thompson

Published by: In Time Publishing & Media Group, 980 North Michigan Avenue, Suite 1400, Chicago, Illinois 60611.

Cover and Layout: J. Sakiya Sandifer of S.T. Grafics - Chicago

Library of Congress Cataloging-in-Publication Data
00-135913

Thompson, Abe My Thoughts Your Journal Our Book

ISBN 0-9704078-0-7

preface

i know my living is making a difference

I wrote this book so my son could read about how I think, and to encourage people to live a more abundant, fulfilling life. Life has so much to offer, if we only take a moment to smell the flowers, to take a deep breath, to laugh and to tell someone you love them.

This book is a collage of information derived from my years of experience as an entrepreneur, motivational speaker, friend, husband and most importantly, father. All of which have nurtured and helped me to live a wonderfully happy life.

If I can, in anyway, help you to live a more fulfilled life, simply by sharing with you my experiences and knowledge, this for me will be another effort to make sure my living has made a difference. I do hope that by reading this book, you too, can come to realize that your existence makes a positive difference in the lives of others.

This is dedicated to the one I love

acknowledgements

For Lovely, my light, my love, my everything.

For Bucket, a lesson, a love, a wonder.

For my parents, Wilma, Marcie and Pete, you are all wonderful.

To Aunt Ovetta.

To Grandaddy (Henry Robinson)

To Pops

To my sister and brothers; Sheryl, Gordon, Michael, Harvey, Rodney, Keith, Jeff and Timmie.

I love you all more than I can express

there are a number of people I need to thank

THE MESSENGERS
Launa Thompson, Samuel Akainyah, Greg Bunch, Melody Spann Cooper;
You said I could do it, and I did. Thanks!

THE WORKERS
Azania Brown (the leader), Betty Hampton, Gwen Washington, Vince Wilkens,
Dequianna Brooks, Sakiya (Sky) Sandifer.
YOUR WORK HAS BEEN AMAZING

To the children I've known and know who have grown up to be great adults.
Mike Applegate, Robert Hayes, Robert Henderson, Malita, Muhammed Ali Jr.,
Marium Ali, Rasheda Ali, Jamilla Ali, Santita Jackson, Angie Bellamy,
Tasha Bellamy, Johnathan Jackson and Jessie Jackson Jr.

To the children I have great hopes for and expectations.
Phoenix, Little Mike, Brittney, Azal, Ankur, Asa, Avery Thomas Moore,
Lil Luin, Christal, Dell, Cody and Stevie, Quinton, Diana, Nubia Murray,
Stephanie Frank and all the kids at Whittier Elementary School.

LEADERS
Miasha Gibson, Theresea Cooper, Dr. Olds, Reverend Jesse Jackson, Launa
Thompson, Oprah Winfrey, Val Gammon, Johnnie Butler, Louisa Storey.
Your leadership by example is so admirable.

THE BELIEVERS
Uncle Preston, Ma and Nap, Earl Dorsey, Henderson, Uncle Joe and Aunt Ellen,
Doris and Bud Mckinney, Mae Brown, Launa Thompson, Anita Rutsky, Mr. Stell,
Mrs. Anderson, Mrs. Caine, George E. Turner, Aunt Margerite.

THE EXAMPLES
Abraham Sr. and Marci Thompson (ma and daddy), Napoleon aand Daisy Gaines,
Sadrud-din and Aminah Ali, Bishop Arthur M. and Mrs. Brazier, Julius and Ruby
Haynes, John and Voya Davis, Matt and Robbie Levy, Ernest and Florence Jones,
Reverend Jessie and Mrs. Jackson, Mr. and Mrs. Eddins, Mr. and Mrs. Glen Olds,
Malcolm and Gloria Hemphill, Stuart and Marlene Rankin, Lynn and Joan Smalls,
Cos and Unita Johnson, Maxine and Bill Leftwich.
I want to be like you. You are all great examples to follow.

For teaching me to ride bears - Searcy "Lee" Montgomery.

To Louis Price and Lenell Hooker for teaching me about following dreams and
for the friendship I can't remember not having.

TO ALL OF YOU . . . YOUR PRESENCE HAS BEEN A BLESSING IN MY LIFE.

chapter headings

Take a look at the books you and your friends have. Are they neat and clean ? or, bent up and loved? You can get a fairly good picture as to their likes and dislikes, their beliefs and non beliefs just by looking at their collection of books. What doesn't impress me however, is when I see a stack of immaculately kept books, each page perfectly crisp and clean, apparent that no-one has read a single page. My belief is that a book should be treated like your favorite hat. A book should be loved, touched, and cared for.

Growing up I was taught never to write in books. I made a great discovery during my first year of college, that it was OK to write in your books. I was absolutely stunned, yet elated. In fact, they actually sold special highlighter pens in the college bookstore, specifically for writing in your book. What a revelation!

'My Thoughts' is literally about 'my thoughts' on a number of things about life and living. The <u>word</u> or <u>phrase</u> at the end of each chapter are to help provoke thought and discussion. In fact, we can discuss that when we meet.

You can use the 'My Thoughts' book in several ways; You can choose to journal your thoughts for <u>self development.</u> There are questions at the end of each segment, you can choose to answer the <u>questions</u> and evaluate your progress as the weeks and months go by. Or, you can simply journal <u>your thoughts.</u> I've even added pages for you to write your thoughts and revelations. The margins are designed extra wide, so that there is enough room for you to jot down notes.

My Thoughts was designed for you to write in your book, in fact I insist that you write in this book. This is your opportunity to let your feelings be known and to let your thoughts be seen, (if you wish). Journalizing your thoughts, experiences and feelings will awaken your subconscious and heighten your thought process, which will in turn help you to focus more on what you want, to appreciate the things you have, and more importantly, love the world you're in! 'My Thoughts' was created to assist you in your journey to a more fulfilling and abundant life.

'My Thoughts Your Journal Our Book' is incomplete without your participation. This is a book that you complete. This book is interactive, so get busy!

PARTICIPATE

I've come to realize that we don't really control anything. We don't control when it's going to rain, sleet or snow. We can't control whether the day goes faster or slower. What we can do is make a variety of plans to fit into the day. How often have you made plans that due to no fault of your own, had to be changed because of say, inclement weather, airport cancellations or illness? If you have been in any of these situations or similar circumstances and were to perhaps give the situation some thought, you would realize a very simple fact, that you don't control the forces around you. A fact that is often taken for granted, especially in a world that has so much technology. Sometimes we try to...and the results turn out to be devastating.

Figuratively speaking, we are all ships. Sometimes we get to dock our ship at a port that we have mapped out. We have weathered the storm, we may have had to put more men on the bridge to control certain aspects of the ship, nonetheless, we made the necessary arrangements to get to the port in one piece and ultimately accomplish our mission. However, depending on the weather conditions, we may not dock our ship in the right port at the right time. We may, for example, dock in Jamaica, when really we wanted to dock in Puerto Rico. Occasionally, we may need to take a diversion, or due to bad weather conditions change course completely.

We may get married, because the right person came along, maybe not at the time originally planned, but the opportunity was right. Or, we may take a job right out of high school, and decide to go to college later. Sometimes, when we chart a course for ourselves, we do not take into consideration the obstacles that may present themselves, obstacles that at the time seem destined to ruin our plans.

As a radio station manager, I had a grandiose ambition to own radio stations all over America. I wanted to own radio stations in major markets, New York, Chicago, Atlanta, Los Angeles and so forth. What a turn of events, that the opportunity to purchase my first radio station did not come from any of those major cities, but from a smaller city, Kalamazoo, Michigan. My first thoughts were, "Is Kalamazoo a real place?" I didn't really know much about the place, nor had I any interest to learn anything about the city. My ego was somewhat deflated. How could I possibly get excited about Kalamazoo, I mean it just isn't New York! I had the most impressive business plan to acquire a major city radio station. I had a team of experts on call, a market analyst, an accountant, attorneys and business strategist, all giving their intellectual opinion on how to make a major radio station successful. As it turned out, I didn't get the opportunity to purchase a station in a major city, in fact, it was Kalamazoo, that was available.
What should I do? Here was a classic example,

of my ship docking in a different port than I had mapped out. I was definitely in the right direction, maybe a little more to the north than I had planned. Should I dock my ship and check out the island to see what it has to offer?, or should I continue on my journey not knowing when I may dock or, if indeed, at all?

I docked my ship at Kalamazoo and can, without hesitation say, it was a wonderful port. I learned so much from owning my first radio station; invaluable experience in acquisitions, radio station ownership and people management. I was able to live out a lifetime dream. I was elated. Everyday was a joy, regardless of the circumstances of that day. I was living my dream, maybe not in New York, Chicago or L.A., but it was my dream brought to reality.

There are a number of ways of looking at a situation. Sometimes it's advisable to let go of all inhibitions about what success really is. Success can be measured in many ways. I would certainly say I was successful in obtaining radio ownership, but, I had to redefine my dream. My dream did not necessarily need to have a specific location, but rather that the core of the dream, being an owner of a radio station, was obtainable. I could absolutely live without the minor details, such as the location of the radio station.

With all the planning I have done in my life, I have come to the conclusion, that unguided ships do port. They may go around in a circle numerous times. Sometimes you may have to check your compass to get a sense of the direction you are going in. But generally, you will get to the port you want to. What often happens is that we make decisions, that affect our docking status. We get to the port, and decide it's not what we are looking for, so before we can even give the island a try, we take up our anchor and sail on. Oblivious to the fact, that the island we just denied ourselves access to, probably held great joy and great experiences.

When we deny ourselves experiences, because they don't measure up to our expectations, we limit our growth and capacity to understand.

The thing about captaincy, is that you realize what type of captain you are. Are you the type of captain to go down with the ship? Are you the type to jump on a life boat as soon as your sailors try a mutiny? Are you the type of captain to look at the map and head to the first island on the map, because you don't possess the patience to go where you would really like to? Or, are you the type of captain that chooses to make a U-turn home at the first sign of a storm.

The type of captain you are determines what course your life will take, and most importantly, the effects your decisions will have on your life.

PATIENCE

What things are you trying to control that you need to let go of ?

What things are within your control that you need to take more responsibility for?

What type of captain are you?

What dreams or aspirations do you have for yourself, and how do you plan to follow your dreams?

Talk to anybody in any part of the world about wealth and most people will talk about money. They understand the importance of money and the power that it yields. They understand that money is able to bring a certain amount of pleasure, take care of some necessities and allow for some freedom.

How many people on the other hand understand the importance of people, and the roles that they play in everyday life? Without people participation we could not do a lot of the mundane everyday duties that we take for granted. We couldn't have that nice cup of coffee at our favorite coffee shop unless the waitress was available to do her job. We wouldn't be able to run into an emergency room at any given moment, if the doctors and nurses weren't willing to accommodate their lifestyles to work different shifts. What if the world was full of people that didn't care what happened to other people? Where would we be?

Many people are spiritually and emotionally bankrupt. They are void of what it really takes to live a successful, fulfilling life, and subsequently raise children with the same void. To really enjoy life and live it to the fullest is to understand that life is made up of precious gems . . . human beings. If you could just imagine that every time you encountered a person, (from any walk of life), it is as though you were to receive a million bucks. How would we react? With a

great deal of respect, no doubt, because then
you would realize what this million dollars could
do for you. Developing good relationships is
better than any amount of money. We should put
a 'priceless' tag on everybody. Having good relationships in life will help you to get the things
you want even if you don't have the know-how or
the finances. People respond to nice people, to
sincere people, to loving people, to respectful
people.

A person with all the money in the world, who
has a bad attitude, in a given situation, can get
less than a person with a good attitude and less
money. My wife and I were returning home
from a trip, I asked the flight attendant quite
politely if we could be upgraded to first class.
The attendant checked the seating arrangement
and obligingly upgraded us to first class. Soon
after, a passenger waving a first class ticket,
arrived late for the flight. He was extremely rude
and obnoxious. The flight attendant explained
the rules concerning arrival times for check-in,
and seated the disgruntled passenger to a coach
seat. Feeling a little disturbed about the situation, I approached the attendant insisting that
my wife and I were willing to accommodate the
passenger with a first class ticket, since we did
not purchase the first class ticket. The flight
attendant insisted that we remain in our first
class seats, and remarked that politeness had
earned us our position.

Treating each person as though they were a million bucks, is surprisingly self rewarding. The feeling of self empowerment, compassion, and a general aura of love will encompass you. When love is demonstrated towards another person, regardless of how difficult that person is, you purge yourself of any negative energy. It's an awesome feeling when someone acts a real ass, and you respond by demonstrating kindness and love in return. You'll leave the situation feeling empowered, and they'll leave the situation feeling disenchanted and powerless.

Courage, integrity, patience and forgiveness are four qualities for a healthy realtionship. To incorporate these qualities in our lives we must unlearn a lot of negative values. We have to be willing to forgive, for example, when we usually hold a grudge and harbor resentment.

Wouldn't it be far more advantageous to the spirit, soul and body, if you treated everybody as though they were a million bucks. If there were some injustice done, it may make them evaluate the relationship.

The key to the 'Everybody's like a million bucks' theory is that when you begin to realize that everyone is extremely valuable, you will have more rewarding relationships.

RESPECT

List the people you value in your life.

How do the people you value enrich your life ?

What can you do to make people feel 'richer' by knowing you?

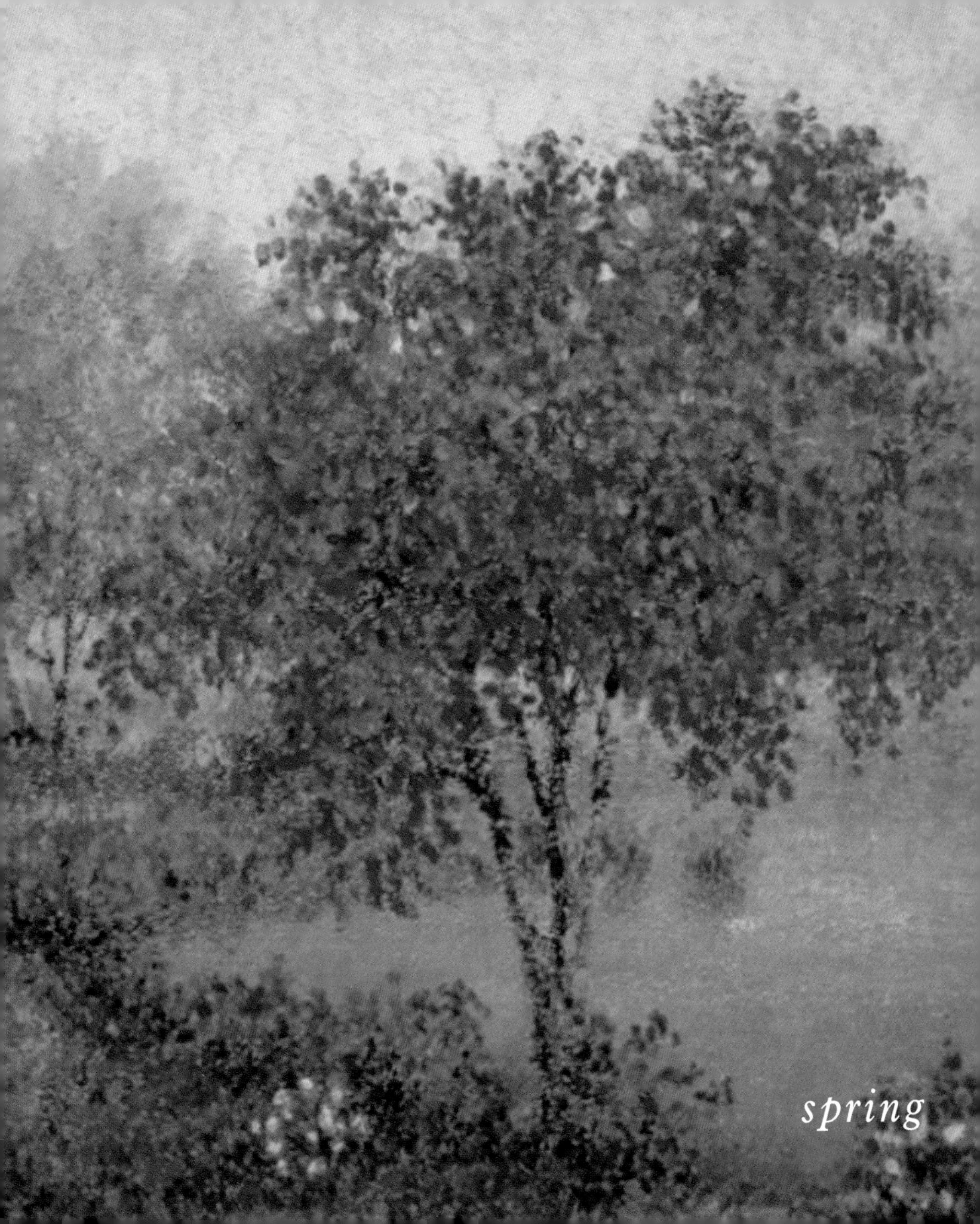

spring

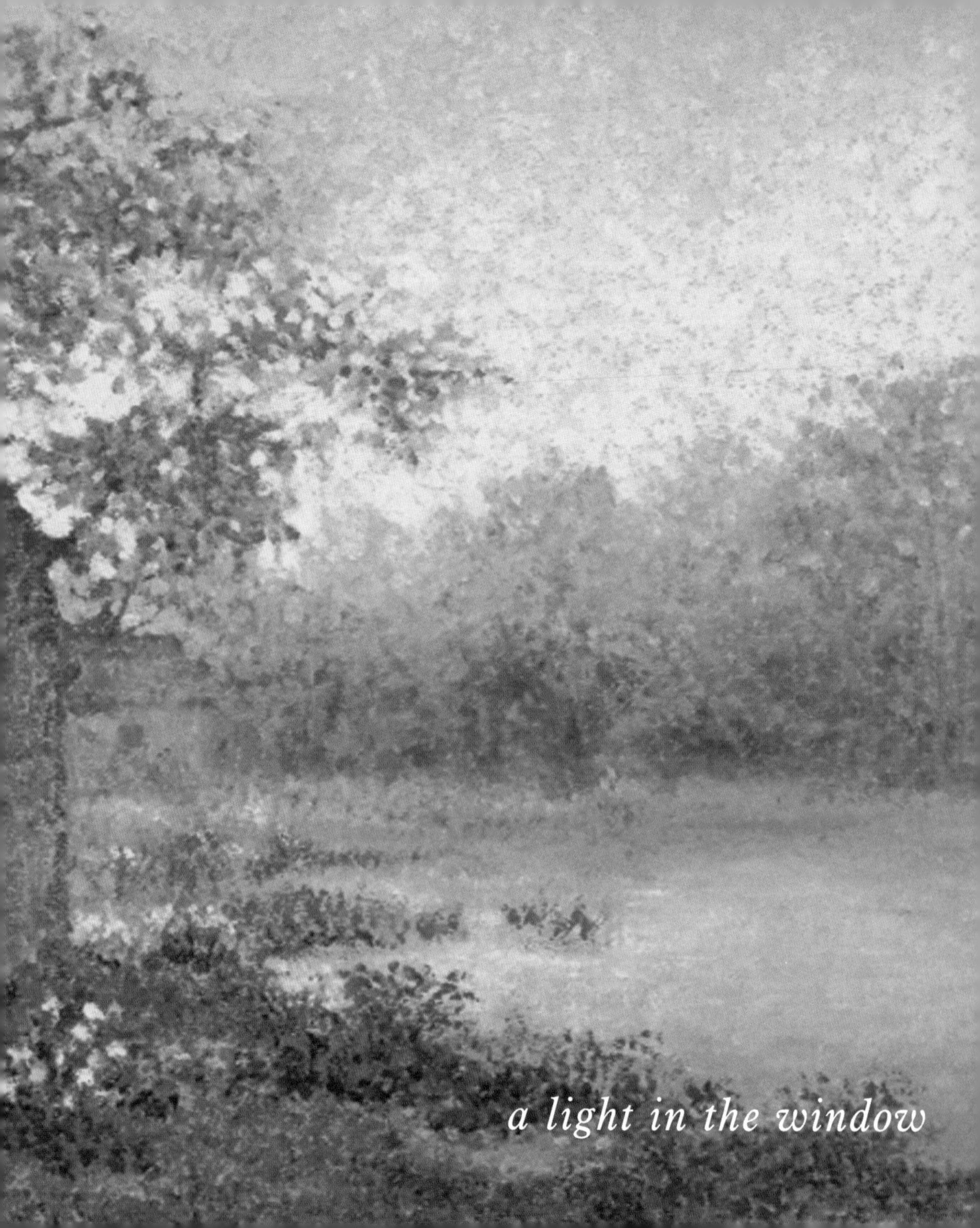
a light in the window

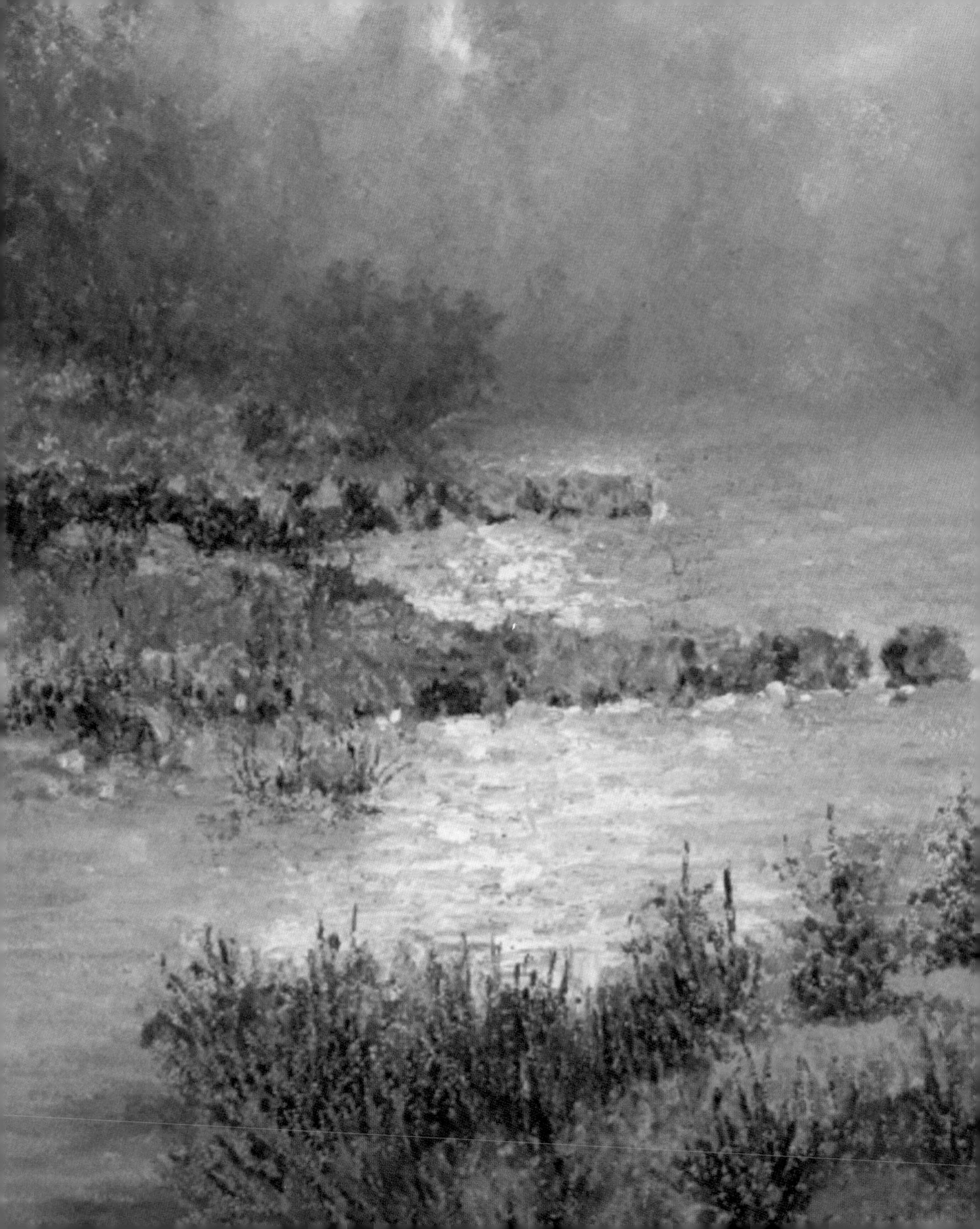

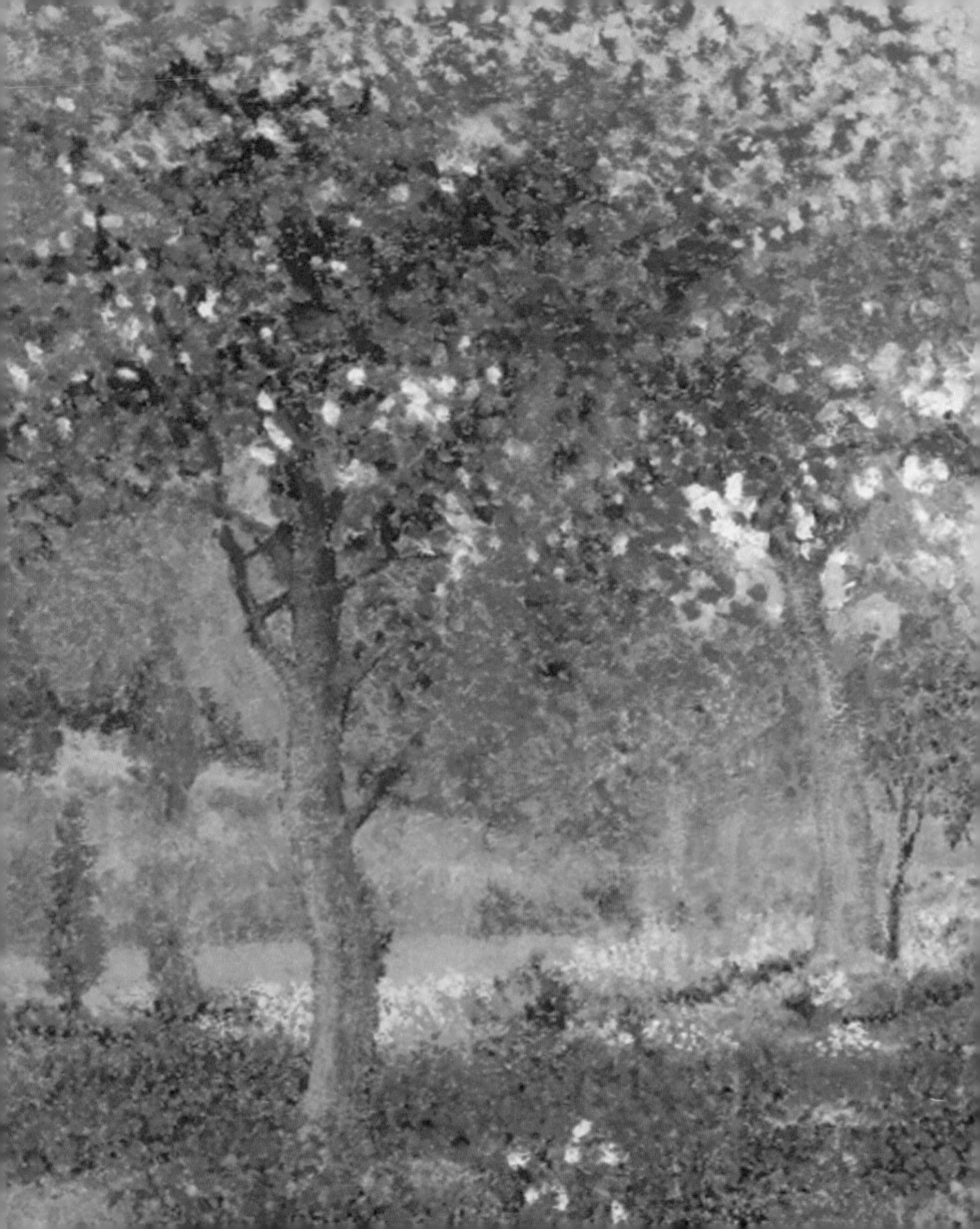

I believe that some adults are the biggest bullies and that children learn their bullying techniques from adults. Some adults bully all the time, some husbands bully their wives and some employer's bully their employees. It's a vicious cycle, perpetrated by insecure people who lack self-esteem but want to feel a sense of power. They believe that by belittling others they empower themselves. Bullying is a way to disguise one's cowardliness. A bully is a person that lives in constant fear. A bully is a tortured person who demonstrates gestures of hate. Bullies hide behind this facade in the hope that they will not be recognized as the whimpering cowards that they are.

In martial arts you are taught about the power of the art form, and the importance of self discipline. A true student of martial arts recognizes that even though life may present combative challenges, he must demonstrate self discipline, not the ability to 'kick butt'. True power is maximized when you don't have to use it or show it.

History reveals that the people we revere the most, the people we admire and respect the most, were the people who demonstrated kindness, love, generosity, patience, courage and forgiveness, e.g; Jesus, Martin Luther King Jr., Ghandi, Mother Theresea, to name a few. Generally, people do not show reverence to bullies or to people with bully like attitudes. We as a people, basically love to love, and love people who demonstrate love.

HUMILITY
19

Do you have any 'bully like' characteristics? List them.

How can you change these characteristics?

List several characteristics that you like about yourself ?

List the things that can enhance you as a person and improve your relationships with others ?

We live in the information age, an age where technology is running rampant. We are judged, not only by our mental and creative skills, but also by our credit report or medical history, and so forth. Our personal information is out there, in information cyberspace, documenting our personal preferences, our spending habits, and even our eating habits. When we order a pizza for home delivery, the information that comes up is mind blowing. The culprit that stores all this information is the good old computer, at your service! A computer data analysts realizes that the most important part of his job is the input of information, because what is put in becomes the blueprint for what will come out. I use the example of the computer, because humans are very much designed in the same way. Only a lot more advanced, more unique and more complex. The human brain weighs an average of three pounds and contains fifteen billion nerve cells, so that you can register every perception, sound, taste, smell, and recall every action. Everything is absorbed through the brain, and stored in our memory banks. We are truly unique, truly powerful creatures.

So in essence, it is true that what we feed our minds, will reflect in our responses, thoughts, actions and deeds. That's why it is so important to monitor the things we say to our children. If you say to a child, "You're so stupid, you'll never amount to much." The child's brain will constantly remind him, "Don't forget you're stupid and you won't amount to much."

Whatever you feed the brain, the subconscious mind will store it, you will become what you think. If you put garbage in, garbage will come out. If you feed your mind with negative material, you'll think negatively, and thus act negatively. We have to learn to prune ourselves, just as we would prune our gardens or our flowers. If you find yourself with garbage thoughts, with self discipline you can begin to prune dysfunctional habits, one at a time. For example, you may recognize in your personality, that you shout at people frequently, your friends, children, partner and workmates. This habit needs some serious pruning. First you have to become aware when you are shouting, and make a concerted effort to speak slowly and quietly. Maybe taking a deep breath will help! Whatever method you choose, (different methods work for different people), you will empower yourself by not responding in a negative way. The feeling of empowerment is a lot more satisfying than uncontrollable behavior. When you slip up, don't beat yourself up about it, dust yourself off, and remember that there was a time when you didn't care about your behavior, now you are a better person for understanding that your behavior is not acceptable, and that you have raised your standards. Learning and practicing self control, is a perfect way to teach yourself better behaviour. Once you overcome a garbage habit, it will be much easier to overcome a second destructive habit, because you will be teaching yourself greater self discipline.

BE CAREFUL WHAT YOU SAY TO YOURSELF

What garbage do you need to get rid of ?

What are your plans to get rid of these negative traits?

Everything in life needs a good foundation, a great city, a building, a career; everything in life has to have a strong foundation. With a strong sturdy foundation, you can grow and develop, and build. This leads us to the understanding that our lives and our lifestyles should be built on a solid foundation.

A construction company may decide to develop a piece of property, an apartment building, or a single family home. The developers know the key is to lay a good solid foundation before they send in interior designers to make the apartment/house look beautiful. Decorating that adds the right shade of carpet and exquisite furniture, is the icing on the cake. The key to the structure weathering the storm is certainly not the furnishings, but the foundation. The foundation is the part that counts the most. In the same way our lives should reflect a good solid foundation. Morals that we can live by, mental and physical stability, a spiritual relationship with god, good health and eating habits are all elements for a strong foundation.

We should teach children at an early age to be kind, sharing, giving, and respectful. Respecting ourselves and others are important qualities for a strong foundation.

A foundation solid enough so that when problems come our way, we are able to return to the lessons that we were taught, to maintain stability. It's our solid rock, our bridge over troubled water, our shoulder to lean on. Our foundation helps to keep us steady, even on what may seem to be the most shaky ground.

ROCK STEADY

Everybody wants to accumulate wealth, but they don't have the right mind set. Some people will play the lottery everyday for three years, win $1000 and jump for joy. Not realizing that they could have put that $1 a day into an account paying 2 or 3% interest, in which case they would have over $1000 in three years. They could give themselves a jackpot!

When it comes down to saving, lack of knowledge could leave you more than a day late and a dollar short.

An investment of $50 a week returning 9% a year would grow after 40 years and gain over a million dollars. If people understand that their chances of winning a big lottery jackpot are probably between 10 million to 20 million to one, they would most likely put their money to better use.

Families can accumulate thousands of dollars through regular savings, if they curtail their spending habits. Billions of dollars are spent each year on unneeded consumption. Just take a look in your local newspaper at all the garage sales advertised each week.

MONEY BEGETS MONEY
If you were to save $2000 a year at 10 percent interest, you will have accumulated $36,000 after 10 years. Then if you took the same initiative and initial investment for another 10 years you will have $126,000. If you keep the same interest rate of 10% for another 20 years, your initial investment will grow to $973,000.

For people who don't know a thing about stocks, a bank will be able to give you details. You can even get a few friends to invest money together to create a stock portfolio. The point is do something!

Your House: If you have a mortgage you can make additional mortgage payments per year and apply it to the principal only, to cut the life of your mortgage in half. It can be a tough financial commitment, but when you weight the benefits against the sacrifice, the benefits win hands down. Paying your mortgage off in the shortest amount of time has many perks, enjoying extra money each month before you retire. More money goes back in your pocket.

Your Rent: Just money you are using to help someone else pay off their property. You get no equity, nor any tax benefits.

Your Bills: Pay off credit cards. You can save thousands of dollars from the interest that you pay on credit cards. When you are out shopping think carefully about your purchases. Give yourself reasons for the purchases. Ask yourself questions, "Is this something I can live without?" Is this another feel good purchase?" There are a number of reasons why people buy unnecessary goods, and there are a number of garage sales each week trying to get rid of unwanted purchases, not to mention all those purchases hanging in closets with price tags still on them. There are a number of ways to accumulate financial wealth, but you have to be willing to make the sacrifices necessary to see your money grow.

I believe that it was Enstein who once said that the most powerful force in the world is compound interest.

SACRIFICE

What item(s) have you purchased recently that you feel you could have lived without?

How much money do you think you can save during a month if you stopped impluse buying?

What ways can you start saving money? How can you invest this money?

GROWTH OF A PENNY DOUBLED DAILY

day	amount	day	amount
1	$.01	17	$655.36
2	$.02	18	$1,310.72
3	$.04	19	$2,621.44
4	$.08	20	$5,242.88
5	$.16	21	$10,485.76
6	$.32	22	$20,971.52
7	$.64	23	$41,943.04
8	$1.28	24	$83,886.08
9	$2.56	25	$167,772.16
10	$5.12	26	$335,544.32
11	$10.24	27	$671,088.64
12	$20.48	28	$1,342,177.28
13	$40.96	29	$2,684,354.56
14	$81.92	30	$5,363,709.12
15	$163.84	31	$10,737,418.24
16	$327.68		

EVERY PENNY COUNTS

A vast majority of things that we take for granted, were once thought of as impossible. Flying in an airplane, talking on a telephone, computers, the internet, to name a few. Imagine discussing the possibilities of the internet with a person, say 25 years ago. They might have thought you were crazy, or thought that they misunderstood you, "What net . . . a fishing net?"

The world is full of impossibilities, that became possible because of someone's bold, courageous thinking. Throughout history there are numerous examples of the impossible becoming not only possible but a part of everyday life, whether in the sciences, sports or arts. Believe in your capabilities, and do not let the negative thinking of others, inhibit your vision or crush your dreams.

Believing in yourself and your God given talents, is the first hurdle in making the seemingly impossible, possible. That's why it is so important that children are given positive encouragement every step of the way. It helps them to develop confidence in their abilities.

The bible teaches, "... As a man thinketh in his heart, so is he", Proverbs 23:7. We are limited only by our thinking!

DREAM

What do you dream about doing?

What things, do you consider impossible, that you would like to do if you had the power?

Look around you, go on, right now, stop what you're doing and take note of your surroundings, the people, the environment. Take a deep breath, and then take a minute to reflect. When was the last time you did that? Taking note of the environment around you and the people who enter your world. Many of us can rarely say we notice much around us. We drive our cars, go to work, look after our families in a semi-conscious state. This semi-conscious state, is a very dangerous state to be in. Not only can it be hazardous to your health, there are a number of people who have had accidents while driving because they were not paying attention to where they were going. Their mind was else-where, they ended up in an accident, and the most surprising thing of all, they wonder how it happened. Nonetheless, being in a semi-conscious state can allow us to miss out on so much of life's most beautiful and spiritually rewarding experiences.

Some people are more conscious about the needs of their car, than the needs of themselves or their families. They can tell you when the car needs oil or when the car needs a tune up. I've even heard people say, "The car has not been itself, I think I need to take it to the garage." Some people are so in tune with their cars, that they can even detect what weather will be too severe for it. Now are these same car enthusiast, as knowledgeable about the people around them, "How's your wife, does she need a vacation?", "Who's your childs' best friend?", "What did your child do in school, today?" They may not be able to answer you as easily as they answered the questions about their car. Why? Because many people are more conscious about their cars than the people around them. These people are emotionally detached, and operate in a semi-conscious state, oblivious to the greatness of life and all it's beauty.

When we live in a semi-conscious state we become reactive instead of being proactive. A proactive person plans ahead, enjoys their surroundings, because they are involved in their experiences. They take joy in everything they do. The reactive person lives in denial. They don't plan. They simply live from day to day, enjoying only a few of their experiences. The reactive person is not satisfied with what life has given them, instead they react with vengeance and bitterness when dealing with their work, home life and social activities. Establishing a good attitude towards everyday things, even repetitive roles/jobs, like taking the children to school, can create a whole, new lease on life. When you take pride in what you do, when you like what you do, it's a lot less exhausting, a lot less demanding.

We may not be able to change the situation immediately. What you can change is the way in which the experience affects you. Take for example, if your daily task is to drive the chil-

*dren to school each morning. You may dread the
experience for a number of reasons, yet the
experience can become rewarding and enjoyable. The key is to take the experience into
another perspective. For example, why not play
music you like in the car on the way to school.
Buy a cassette or CD of the music that makes
you feel happy, or music that brings back fond
memories of a particular period in your life. You
may even decide to share the experience with
your children, and allow them to play their
favorite music in the car, maybe once or twice a
week. You will find the experience rewarding,
and satisfying. It may solidify a more understanding and loving relationship between you
and your children.*

*This small principal applies to everything.
Having the ability to find positive aspects, in
situations that may be displeasing to us, will
ensure that life is less taxing and more enjoyable.*

SEIZE THE MOMENT

What things in your everyday life do you need to pay more attention to?

How can you make your life a more enjoyable experience?

Count the Squares

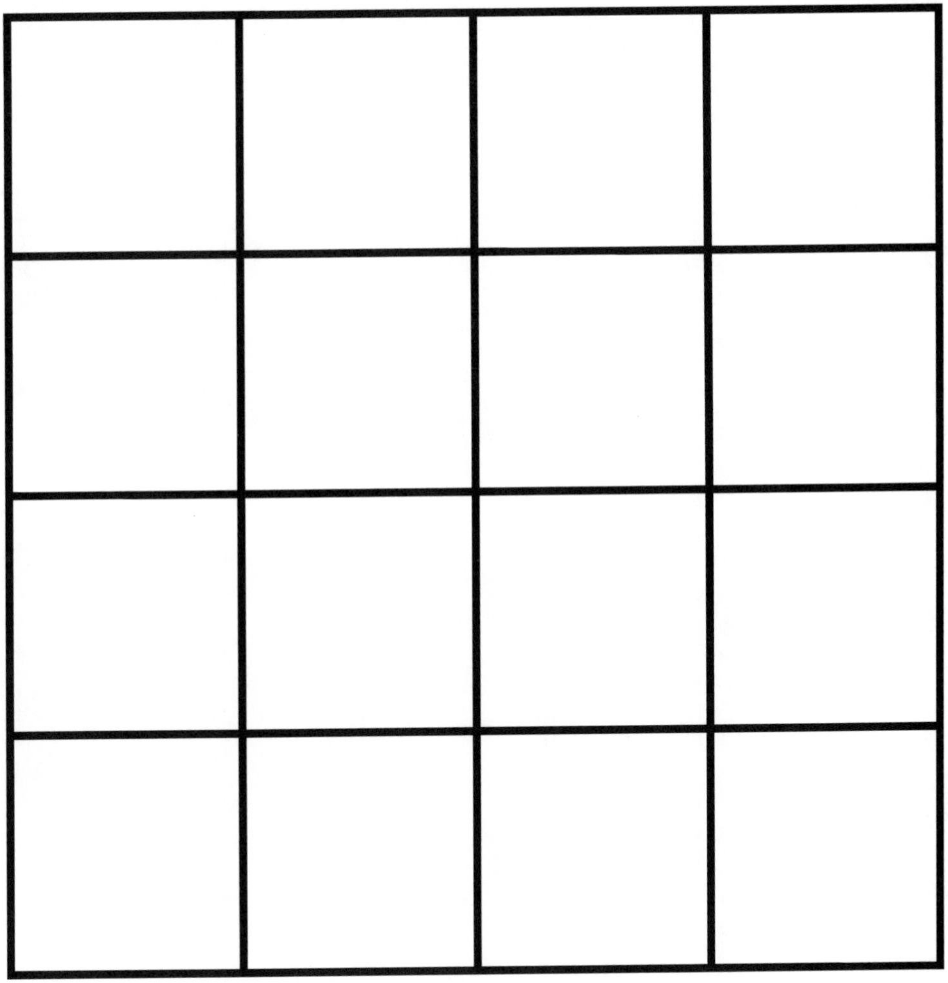

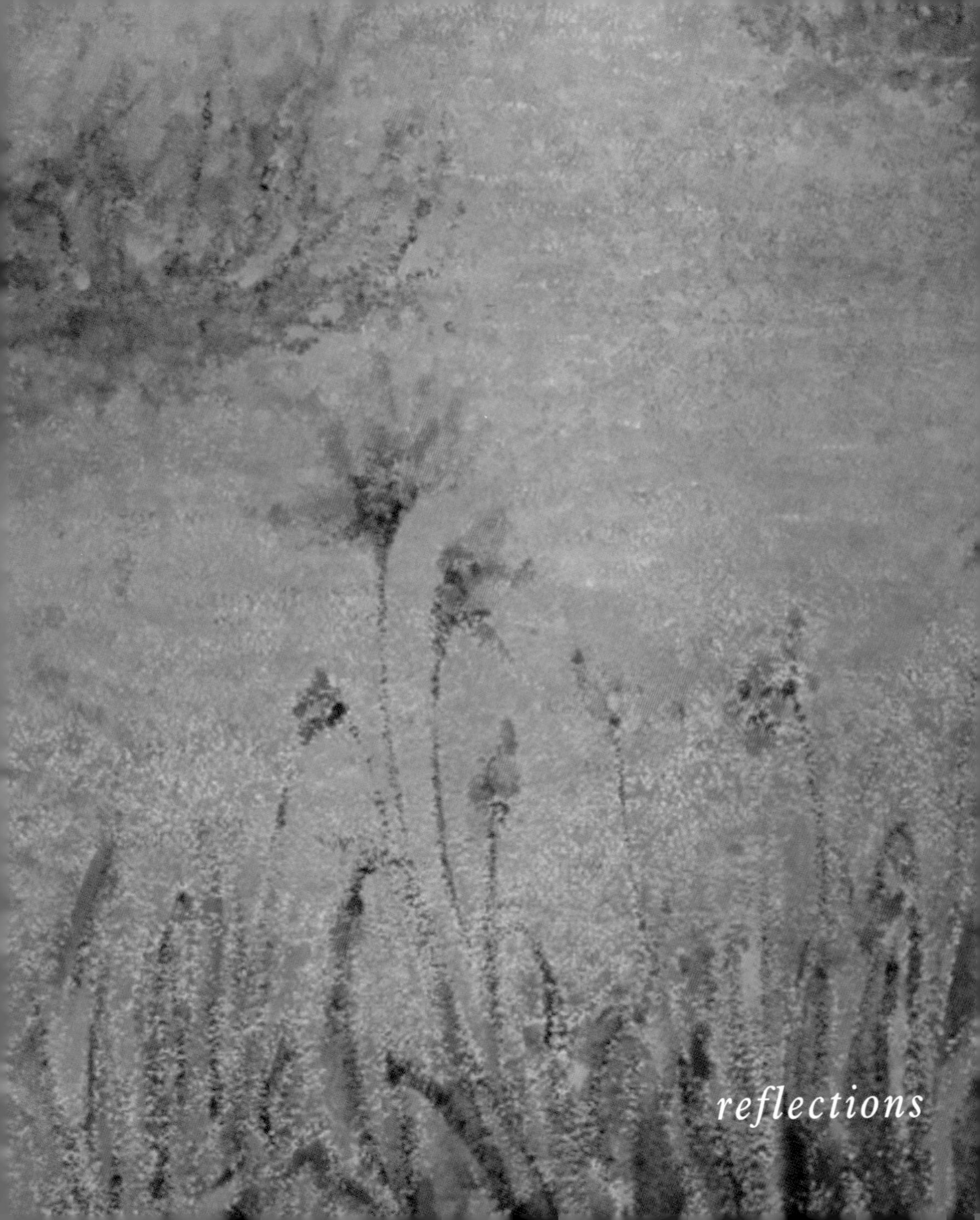

reflections

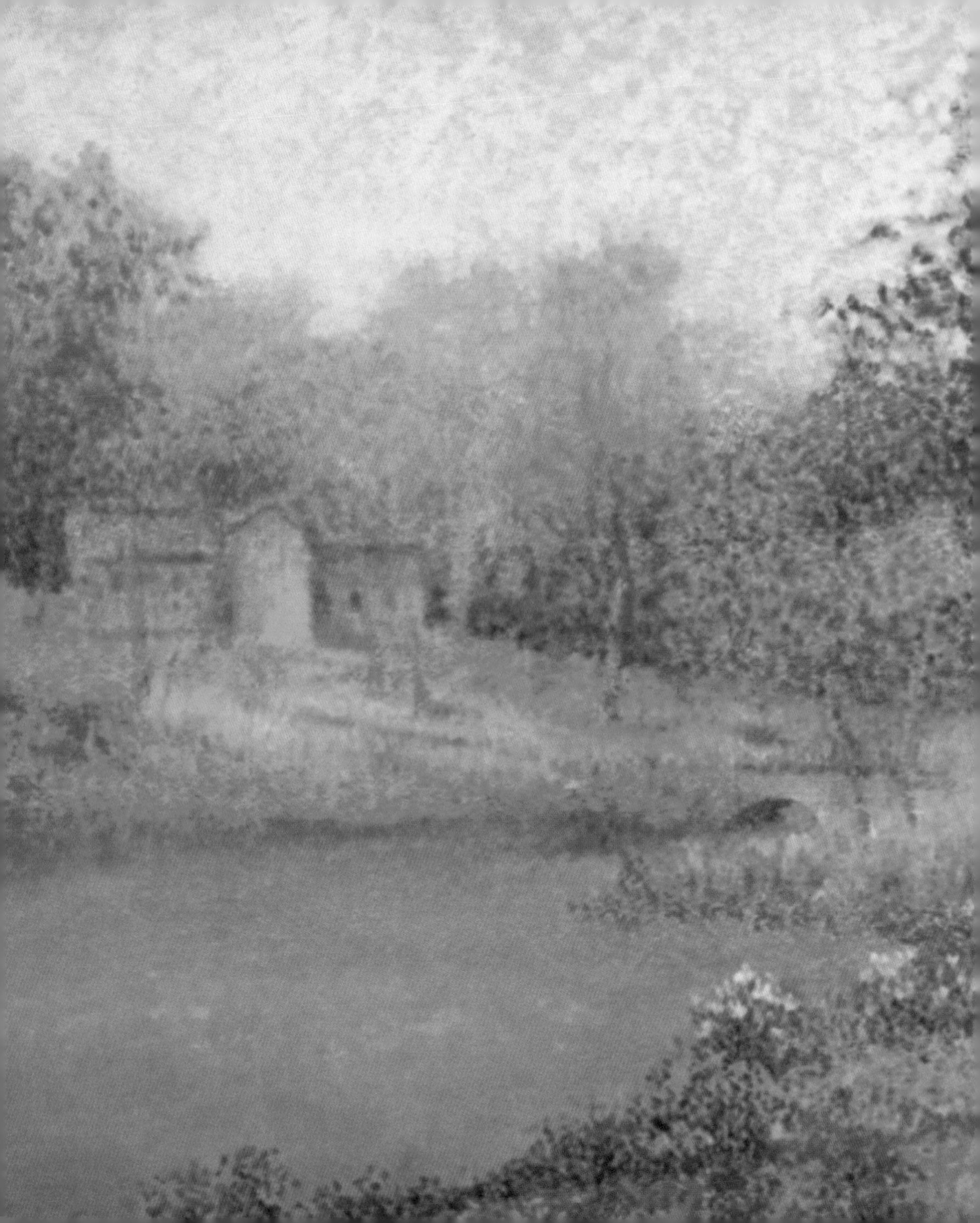

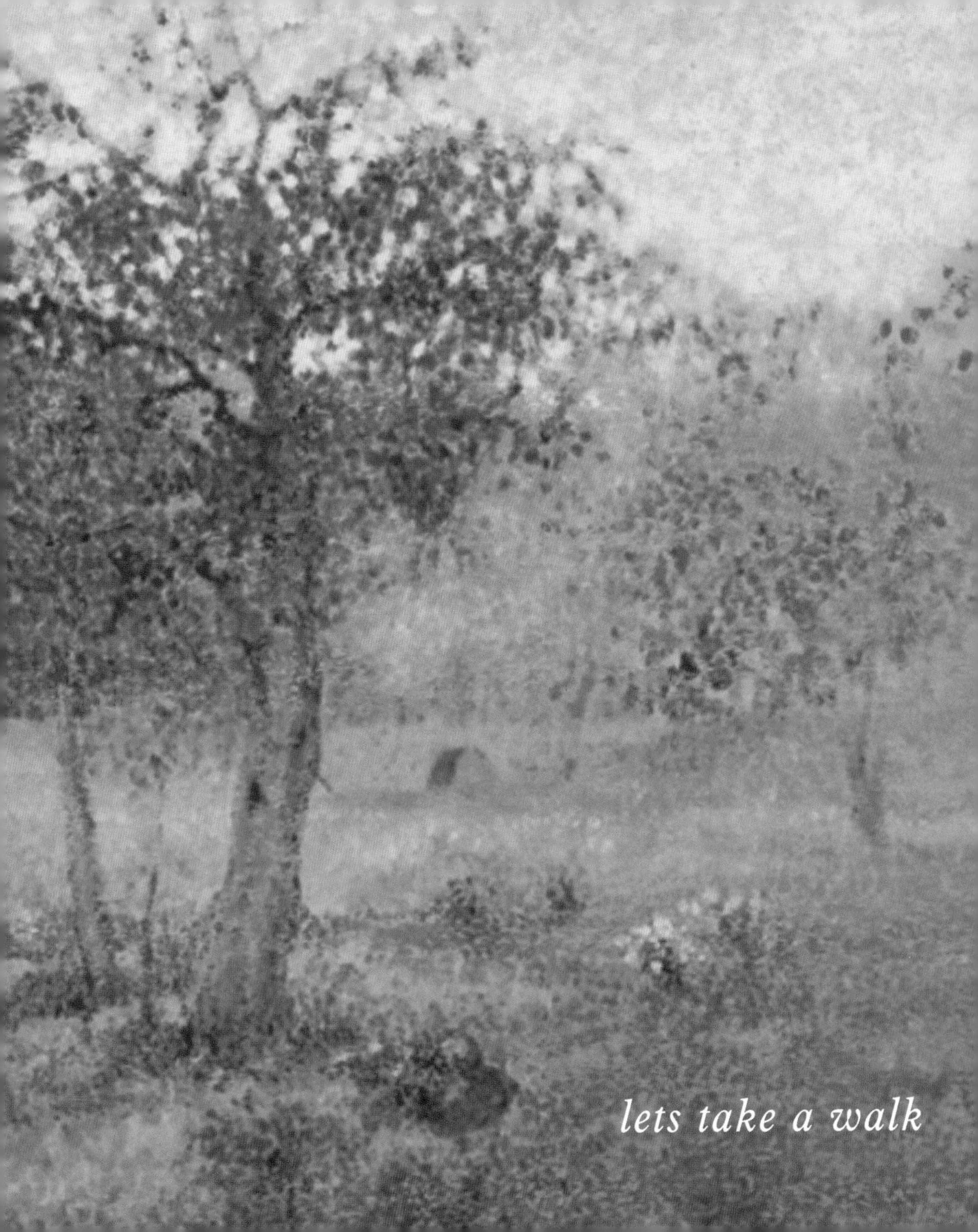
lets take a walk

Your mind is so powerful. If you can't visualize yourself being an educated person, then more than likely you won't become educated. Visualization is the key to making your dreams reality. The theatre of the mind is more powerful and impactful than any movie screen. Imagination and visualization are so important in what your reality will be, and the kind of experiences you will have. How many times have you heard people say that the book was better than the movie? Even with all the Technicolor, special visual and 3D effects, the book wins hands down. That's because the mind can take us to any place in the world, imagine any scenario, and conceive great things. The mind is the best D.V.D. special effects cinema we will ever have. Can you imagine what will happen when you put your mind to positive use. You need to stop looking at a overwhelming situation or problem in a negative way, and put the mind into "Positive" gear. Visualizing how you want your life to be and the type of people you want in your life, is the key to a better life. You would then be the author, director and producer of your own life. You could then relinquish fear and drive full speed ahead to a successful, fulfilling life.

It's important to see yourself doing what your heart desires to do. It's imperative that you spend a few minutes a day visualizing in the theatre of your mind, your dreams and desires. The mind is fertile soil, and your imagination is the seed. Be diligent about watering the soil everyday, and get ready to see what happens. If you can't see it in your mind, you can't see it in life! You can't see what you can't see!

MAKE YOUR OWN MOVIE

What things do you need to look at differently?

What can you do today to bring you a step closer to your dream?

(Make an attempt every week to do something towards achieving your dream.)

you can't see what you can't see

count the squares

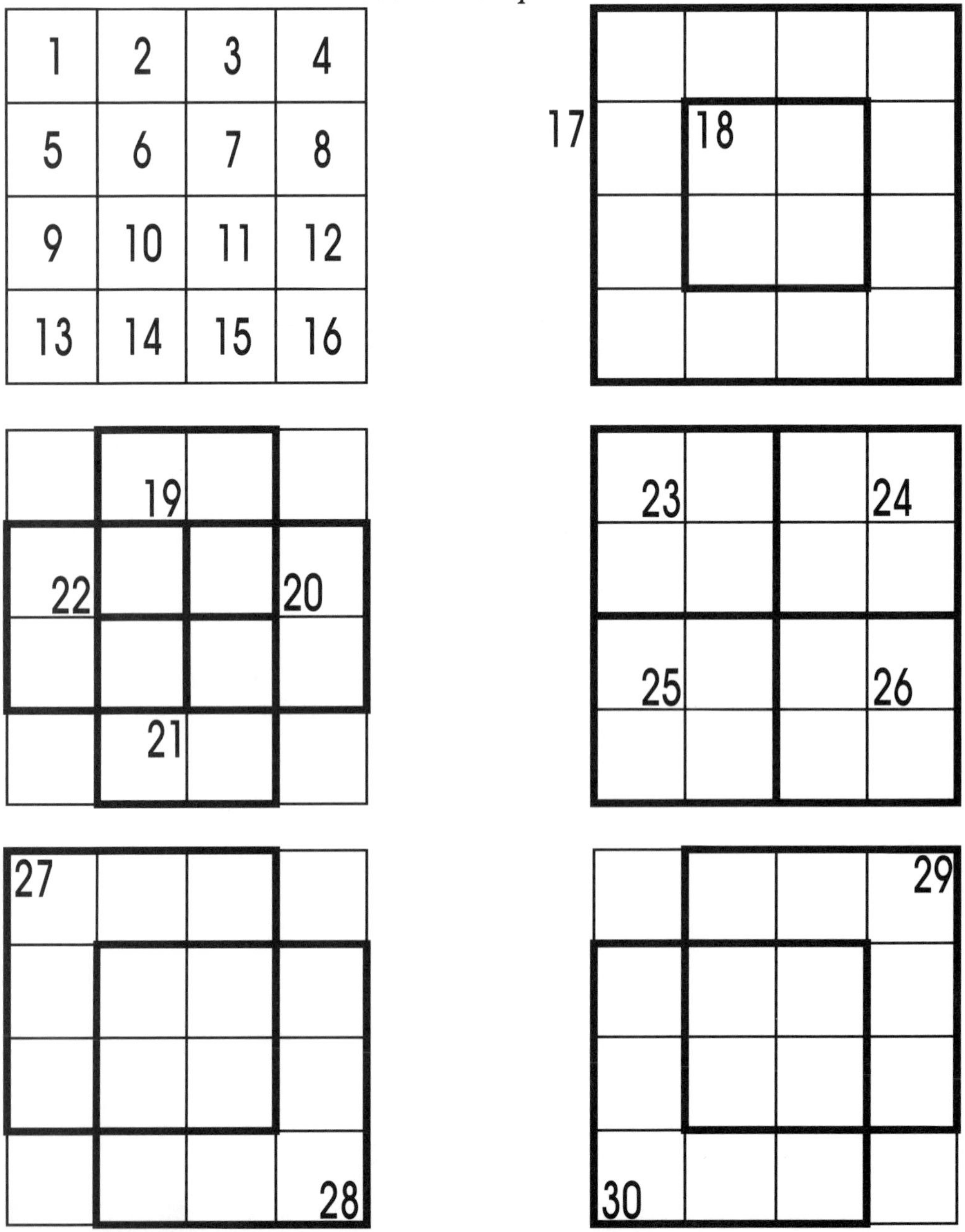
1 2 3 4
5 6 7 8
9 10 11 12
13 14 15 16
17
18
19
22
20
21
23
24
25
26
27
29
28
30

It is often said that we shouldn't have fear. I don't agree with that, because I think fear can help you make decisions about what you should or should not do. How you deal with fear is more significant than fear itself. When you recognize that you have fear, and that fear is holding you back from participating in life as you should, then you can help yourself deal with the fear head-on. Subsequently when you are prepared to take the first step forward to address fear, then you are putting the ball back in your court. You become the decision maker, instead of allowing fear to make all the decisions for you.

Before I started motivational and public speaking engagements, I always harbored a fear of speaking before crowds. It didn't matter if it were a large or a small crowd. With a sincere will to overcome my fear, I constantly challenged myself, pulling the courage from within, to deal with the fear logically. When there is an innate fear of something, one has to ask the question "Why am I fearful?"

There are three steps to understanding and overcoming fear; *INFORMATION*, *BREAKDOWN* and *EMBRACE*. *INFORMATION*: It's wise to learn about the fear in question, read books on it, listen to self help tapes, speak to people who may have had the same problem in the past, surf the internet for associations or groups that have information on the fear. Because the more you know about fear, the greater your chances of disarming it. *BREAKDOWN*: Now you know what *causes fear and where it comes from, break it down. Ask yourself what you can do to disarm the fear you have. Sit in a quiet area, and meditate on the reasons that caused the fear to develop. <u>EMBRACE</u>: Now you know where the fear comes from and how it started. Embrace it. Challenge the fear. Make your mind up. Tell yourself that you are your own boss, and that you are no longer going to allow fear to take charge. Come up with solutions to deal with the specifics of the fear. Sometimes when we admit we have a fear of something, we immediately relinquish that fear powerless. Fear becomes negative when people run away from it. When you end up not accomplishing tasks because of fear then it is time to address that fear head-on. The key is to face fear, gain an understanding of it and move on.*

Fear can be overcomed . . . you must have a fearless attitude to deal with it. Even now I may admit to an audience that I am nervous or fearful, but I face my fear and move on.

KNOWLEDGE

What are your fears?

List five things you can do to overcome each fear.

When a person has admirable traits, for example being kind, sincere, honest or giving, these are characteristics that need to be harnessed, developed and nurtured. Whatever positive attributes exist within an individual, they should be kept in the temple of the soul, protected and available, to unleash when they are needed.

In the pursuit of a goal, regardless of how big or small it is in the opinion of others, surrounding yourself with positive people is imperative. Being in relationships that fully exercise your gifts, is optimum for positive growth. Positivity will reinforce itself. You may set a goal for yourself which is quite challenging, but with the right people around you, giving you positive feedback, that same goal may not appear so odious. Their support, encouragement, or shoulder to cry on when necessary, are the ingredients that set positive people in a league of their own. Negative people do not have any thing to offer, except negativity. Negative people, if given the opportunity, will drown every creative idea in a cesspool of doubt, anxiety and fear. It's like putting a vibrant plant in poisonous soil. If you can't change the people around you.....you need to change the people around you.

IT IS GOOD

Who are the positive people in your life?

Who do you feel are the negative people in your life, and why?

What can you do to surround yourself with more positive people?

Some people think that there are only two guarantee's in life; death and taxes. There are, however, more powerful guarantee's in life, and they require no deposit. We are guaranteed a quality life. Providing we are willing to believe and accept that we are guaranteed a quality life. We have but to make one contribution, and that is our conscientious effort to appreciate all that surrounds us. An appreciation, for example, as basic as a flower or a tree, the sky at night, city buildings, people of all backgrounds, our families and friends. To understand the importance of appreciating all that encompasses our world, will ultimately lead us to a better quality of life. Everything is an important experience. You decide whether you have a good life or not. It's a guarantee that is very rare, because unlike death and taxes, you are the immediate decision maker. There is nothing anyone can do to stop you from having a more fulfilling, abundant and happy life.

Appreciating lifes' riches helps to enhance our spiritual and emotional wealth. Another guarantee, not recognized by many people is the accumulation of wealth. We can all guarantee that we accumulate wealth. It takes discipline and focus. But regardless of one's financial situation, amassing wealth can be a sure thing. Take the example of Osol McCarthy, who throughout her entire working life made less than minimum wage. Ms. McCarthy, accumu-

lated a total of $150,000 in savings, of which she decided to donate to a college, in light of her great respect for God, education, and youth. If an individual is able to save $10 a month, by the end of the year they would have saved $120. Making them $120 dollars wealthier than at the beginning of the year. Many people don't respect quarters and dimes, and so their money will not respect them.

Don't let your money come in the left hand and leave out in the right hand.

BELIEVE AND RECEIVE

List ten things in your life that you appreciate?

List the ways you can make your life a more fulfilling experience?

If someone said they had a very unique gem for you that was rare, that there wasn't another like it on the face of the earth. What would you say? What would you do? How would you react? My guess is that you would be thrilled, excited, even elated at the potential prospect of this gift. You would probably cherish this gift, protect it from all forms of danger, and watch everyone to make sure it isn't stolen. Some people have come to the conclusion that having children is burdensome. They will consider everything from the cost of living, to school fees, to a limit on their social life. Having children from their perspective is a trade-off with a 'having it all' life. How wrong these people are. Those views are plagued by misconceptions, more often than not, in and from childhood experiences, which have contributed to a sense of selfishness.

Let's consider a few benefits, normally I say, "Perks Of The Job" 1; As a parent the involvement with a child allows you to experience unconditional love from another human being. 2; Children give love instantaneously, there are no conditions to their love. 3; A child's' love cannot be bought by the highest bidder, nor destroyed by a cruel, callous act. 4; Children will love you regardless of your imperfections.

You never know who your child may grow up to be. Your child could be a doctor who discovers a treatment for a deadly disease, or the next great athlete, musician, humanitarian, politician, lawyer or entertainer. When we view chil-

dren as "The next big thing", we are more appreciative of their presence. Then you will be saying, with a proud glee in your eyes, "That's my child!"

Imagine being able to say that your daughter or son accomplished great things in this life. Imagine the feeling when this same child turns around and acknowledges you, as one of the greatest influences in their life. The reward of rearing, productive children is priceless. The joy received by developing this life and from sharing your life, is incomparable.

NURTURE

Are you nurturing enough to the child(ren) in your life?

How can you become a positive role model in a child's life?

What can you do, or how can you participate, in an association or charity who target the needs of children?

There are some very special people in this world, and many of us know at least one of them. They are unique because they seek to make life a better experience for all they meet. They are giving people, who always have time to listen, always willing to help in any way they can. They are the personification of human love, because their spirits are still childlike in that they love unconditionally. The problem arises when we meet these people, we don't know how to appreciate them. Some of us even take advantage of their kindness, and some of us because we have been hurt by other people, refuse to give these special people a chance. We find it hard to believe that people can be so kind, so sincere, but we need to take a chance and believe them, for we might gain something from the experience.

Life is full of experiences, some of which can be painful. However, we must learn from these experiences. No experience is in essence '"bad", it is just another tool of life to help us to learn and grow.

If you look at experiences as an opportunity to learn and grow, then you won't harbor feelings of resentment and distrust. Sometimes we should run the risk of being hurt. We should let go of all the negative attitudes that keep us from enjoying healthy relationships.

When we meet people that are giving and sharing, welcome them. Accept them for who and what they are . . . receive the positive energy they give. These people are special only because they realize that it is better to be giving and loving, than to be uncaring and selfish.

Name five people you know who are giving individuals. How can you show these people you appreciate them?

How can you be more giving?

People often limit themselves, other people and all the wonderful possibilities in life, because they spend too much of their time judging. More often than not, these same people, make the wrong judgements about people they don't even know, and so limit themselves from the interaction gained from accepting people as they are. Whether you agree with someone or not, you may not like the color of their hair, the style of their dress, the tone of their voice. Regardless of those realities or perceptions, no one under any circumstances should judge another. There is not one person under the sun that is without imperfections and insecurities. There is not one person living that hasn't made mistakes, (and that's a good thing, because we learn from our mistakes...if we are smart). When we judge someone, we are unconsciously saying, "I am better than you," and let us be frank, there is no one better than the other. We are all equal in the eyes of God. Judging has become an epidemic in our society, we are constantly being judged by others and we are constantly judging others.

We thrive on the prospect that there is someone out there that we are better than, so we judge and judge indiscriminately. We judge without care and consideration of someone's right to be an individual. How wonderful it would be if we didn't judge people. Instead, we allowed each individual to live according to their wishes. We could learn so much more from interacting with people that we normally would sit back from a distance and judge. We can all learn from one another. One thing for sure, life would be more interesting, enlightening and rewarding.

APPRECIATE

Do you find yourself judging others? If so why?

How can you be more appreciative of the differences in people?

To love and love unconditionally, is perhaps the most precious gift we can give. When we choose to love someone, we should make this choice on the premise that we do not expect anything in return. Love is priceless. Children are our best examples of unconditional love, and we should take the opportunity sometime to really study children. Try and recreate that child like personality, strive to be open and free. Be free to love and receive love.

When you allow yourself to become vulnerable, when you let go of all inhibitions, loving becomes exhilarating and fulfilling. When you get to a point in a relationship where it truly becomes loving, intimacy develops, and you feel liberated...because in essence, it feels good to love. When we demonstrate love we demonstrate the presence of God.

To maintain a loving relationship, it is paramount to avoid unnecessary confrontations. In short, don't sweat the small stuff. In my opinion it is more important to be happy than to be right. Being able to discuss differences respectfully, is like fertilizer to a plant. Your relationship will flourish and grow healthy. Loving relationships need constant attention. Your thoughts should always focus on how you can make the relationship more loving. Things you can do or say, no matter how small, can make your partner or loved ones feel special and certainly, more loved. In doing so, not only will you have more enjoyable relationships, every aspect of your life will be enriched. Why? Because it's hard to love part time. You will become a more loving person, with a loving perspective to life. To love is an innate part of our being and with a little practice, will trickle down to all aspects of our lives.

LOVE

How can you be more loving?

Do you feel loved? If so why, and if not, why not?

The benefits of positive thinking cannot be over emphasized. To think positively gives you the power to take control of a situation. Positive thinking is perhaps, one of the most influential forces that you have dominion over. Many prolific events in our history happened because someone thought positively. They did not get lost in the circumstance or the situation, but set their goals and then put positive thinking into first gear. Madam Currie, Jessie Owens, Dr. Charles Drew, Lena Horne, Dr. Joh Hope Franklin and Sonny Bono, all faced adversity in one form or the other, yet, their positive influence, lives on.

Although positive thinking is an asset that we all possess, very few utilize it. Whatever the reason, negative experiences in childhood, low self-esteem, it is never too late to implement a new strategy in your thinking. The 'new positive' habit may take a while to take root in your mind, remember, you have been thinking negatively nearly all your life, however, practice makes perfect. Once you become aware of your thinking patterns, it's then easy to implement a new effective 'positive' thinking process.

Positive thinking gives emotional and spiritual wealth. It is my belief that schools should teach their pupils the benefits of positive thinking. Then they will mature into positive thinking adults, thus making the world a better place.

Let's face it, how we think shape our lives. The mind is the most powerful entity known. Everything starts in the mind!

THINK

What situation in your life would you like to make more positive?

Write it down. Start thinking positively today!

There are times when the past should be exactly that...the past. When you live in a time warp, reminiscing about negative experiences, harboring on what negatives have been said about you or done to you, although these experiences are past, they are constantly molding your future. Basically, if you can't learn to bury the past, you'll find yourself buried in it.

Nothing good comes from holding onto negative experiences. Some people relish negative experiences. They will make references to the past "Nobody will ever do that to me again. I"ll make sure of that", or "I'll never trust anyone again." We go through experiences for learning benefits. If we accept each experience from the standpoint that we are a better person because of it, then it won't matter so much if the experience is positive or negative. Rather, our lives are enriched based on what we were able to learn.

Being honest and open to oneself about the past is imperative for spiritual and mental growth. We have to be able to look in the mirror and like what we see. We have to take a look at our past, acknowledge it for what it was, learn from it and move on. When we can do this, we can truly bury the past, live in the present and plan for the future.

Food For Thought: A positive attitude can make a good experience better and a negative experience better. But a negative attitude will make a good experience bad and make a bad experience worse.

ONWARD

What do you need to bury?

What can you learn from some of your negative experiences?

The human experience is so involved and varied. Emotions, the situation, timing and experience all play an important part in our decision making process. Sometimes people respond in a way that is negative because they are simply having a "bad" day. If you approach someone on one of their so called "bad" days to make a critical decision on say for example, a business venture, or an idea of some kind, this person may not be in the mental frame of mind to receive your idea. Don't be put off by people's moods or attitudes. There should never be an excuse for accepting someone's negative attitudes. If you do, you're giving someone the power to make decisions in your life and for your life. You are the ultimate decision maker. You create your destiny. Learning to read between the lines of what people say will help give you a better understanding of a personal situation. Ask people how they feel and what they would really like you to do. You have to be assertive, alert and conscientious enough to understand with whom you are dealing. This takes practice, but once you become accustomed to dealing with people and their different personalities, you're half way to winning the prize. As you study life and people, you'll come to realize that all are constantly selling. Life and "the big sell" are interrelated. Everybody sells at some level, even children. A child may see a toy advertised, and must decide how to get someone to purchase it. The first thing a child will consciously plan, is when will there be a good time to ask someone about this new toy. The child will tell you all about the toy, all the features it has, where you can get it, and most importantly, why he/she should have it. If a child detects that you are not in a good mood, or perhaps too busy to respond positively about purchasing the toy, what does the child do? The child will make a conscious choice to make his/her request known at a more appropriate time. Why?.....because even a child can recognize that No can mean Yes later. So they'll approach the situation at a better time. Children understand the importance of persistence.

NO COULD MEAN . . .
- You haven't given me enough information
- It is not a good time
- I don't think you've done enough work
- I don't feel comfortable enough

PERSISTENCE

How can I make my request more acceptable?

What things must I find out about a person prior to selling them on a concept or idea ?

You're familiar with the phrase, "A little kindness goes a long way," but how many people actually show a little kindness each day. We would all have a different outlook on the benefits of kindness if we could only see the immediate rewards of our efforts. Imagine if you could look into a crystal ball, to see where each act of kindness would lead. Imagine that each act of kindness was rewarded, not necessarily by the person who received the kindness, but by an unexpected individual, who in turn, doubled the kindness shown. What would you do? Would your attitude towards demonstrating kindness change?

Kindness is a member of the love family. The importance of illustrating kindness in our everyday life, means that we can easily facilitate loving relationships. Which ultimately catapults us into a secure state of being. We become content with ourselves and those around us. Showing kindness empowers us, we put ourselves in the drivers seat of life, in that we take control of situations by controlling the energy that we send out into the universe. Kindness is a positive energy and when we make a concerted decision to show kindness to others, we are much more likely to receive it in return.

GIVE

What 5 random acts of kindness will you perform in the next week, for people you know?

List 5 random acts of kindness you will perform in the next week, for someone you don't know, and for which you will not receive any credit.

The only way that you will not experience death, is if you have never lived. Passing on is inevitable and should be handled with the same amount of consideration and planning as is needed when you are buying a house, a car or starting a family. You wouldn't let someone decide what you are going to wear to your wedding, so why would you let them decide what you wear on your final day in this life.

When you pass on you will not be able to partic-ipate in any of the funeral arrangements, so why not decide how you would like to be prepared in advance. Your friends and family will be saddened at the loss, but wouldn't it be nice to relieve them of the stresses involved in your passing! At best a persons passing often leaves relatives and friends financially drained and emotionally crippled. If you pass on without leaving written instructions about your prefer-ences, state law will determine who will have the right to decide how your 'stuff' (business) will be handled. Usually the government recognizes the following as legitimate persons as decision makers; spouse, child/children, parents, next of kin, or at worst a public administrator.

At the very least you should write a note about what to do with your belongings, no matter how much or how little you have. You can even leave your loved ones personalized letters, describing how you want to be remembered by each and everyone. Or, maybe you could leave them something to lighten the mood on what is normally considered a sad time, leaving instruc-tions to organize a brunch, lunch or buffet at your favorite restaurant, or for the those who have a lot of money, perhaps you could treat your loved ones to a gateway at your favorite holiday retreat. Trust me they will be sad to see you go, but will love the sentiment that you thought about them in advance. I think it is wise to carefully consider where you want your money to go, and if at all possible, give the money away to those you wish to benefit from it, before you move on. Not only will you be around to appreciate the hearty 'Thank You', but you will be able to see where your money is going and who it is benefiting. Planning for the inevitable includes other things, such as getting to know your family and friends better. Very often people are so caught up with materialism, that they forget about meaningful relationships, that need to be established and cemented while you are alive. We should use time wisely, to enjoy relationships, and to establish bonds that are strong enough to transcend this life. Forgiving is paramount, because a lifetime from now grievances and resentments will seem foolish. One of the keys to a happy life, is to realize that you will have differences with others, and that's all they are, differences of opinion. Life goes on. We aren't expected to agree with everyone about everything. With planning, the inevitable can be an enlightening journey, where loved ones can remember you in peace and serenity. If we are assertive enough to plan in advance, we will leave our loved ones

*knowing they had the privilege of remembering
an individual, who after all, was unique, and who
planned for their own journey.*

So live (and love).

PREPARATION

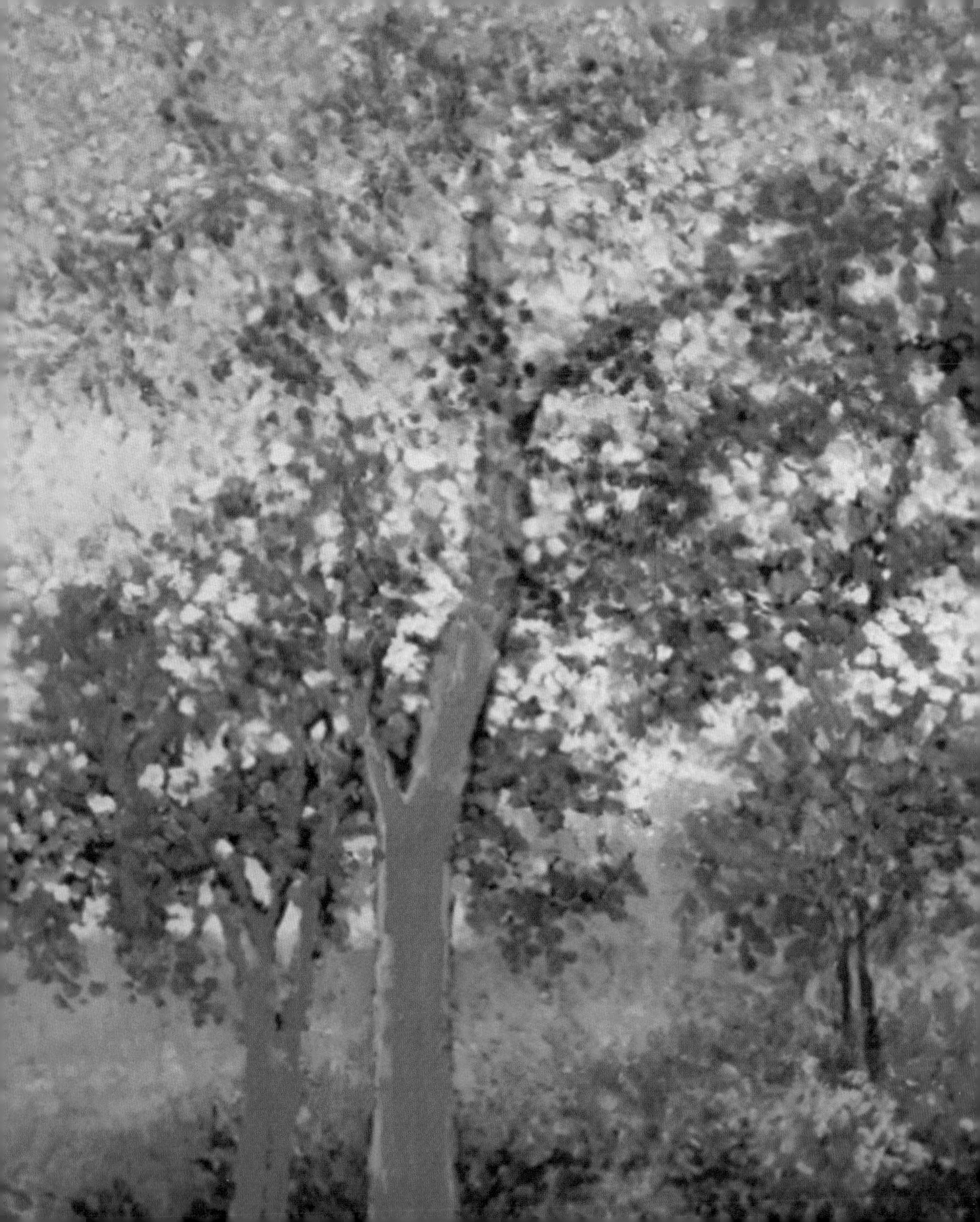

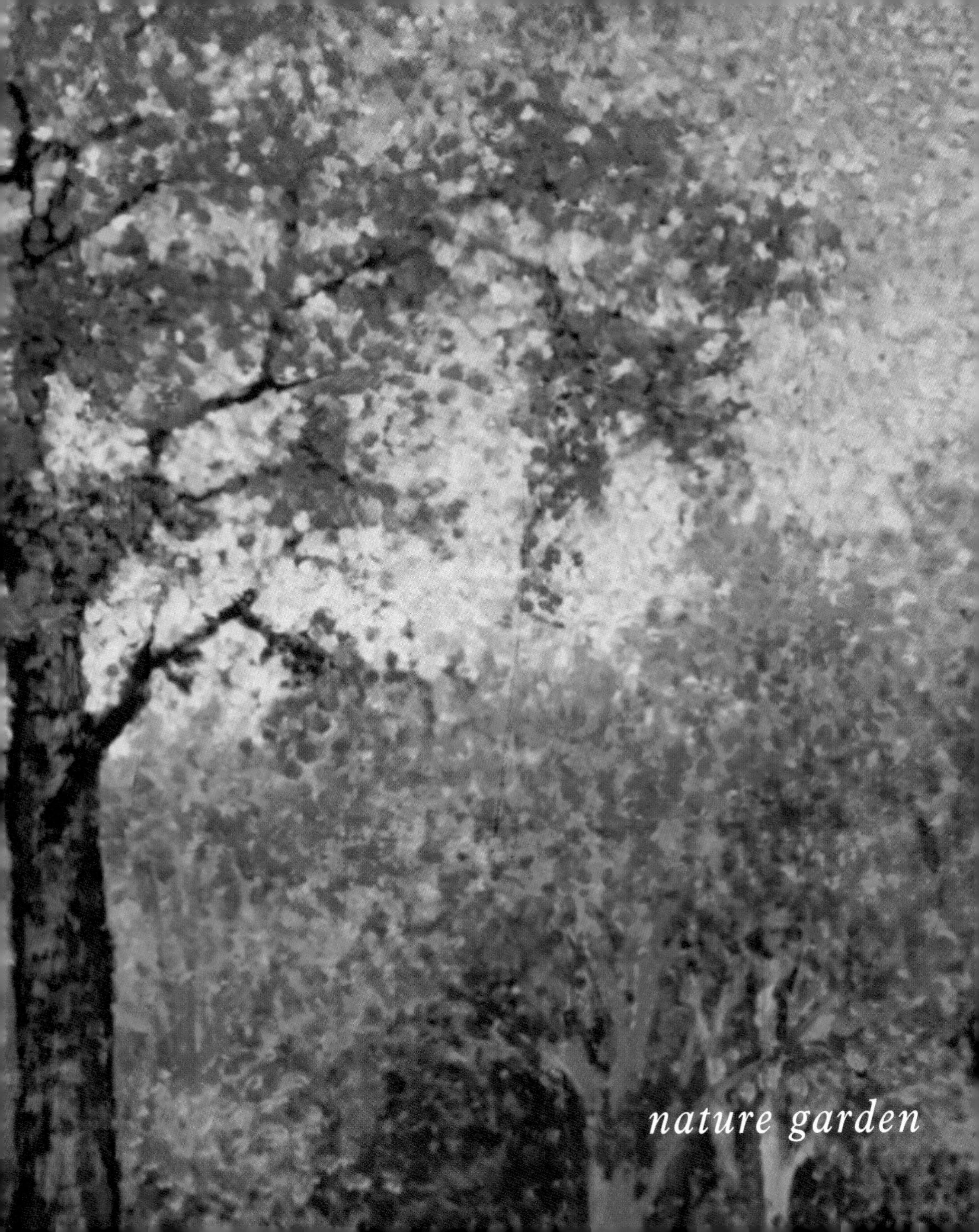

nature garden

the gentle water of god

You cannot bask in your success nor wallow in your failure. Why? Because both are but fleeting moments in time. The real focus should be on the moment, how to cherish it, learn from it and enjoy it. For whether you are experiencing success or failure, they are both times in which you can learn more about yourself and your abilities. Cherishing your accomplishments and learning from your failures no matter how great or small, will help to keep your feet firmly on the ground.

When you are successful, it is important to remember where you came from, and not assume that you are better than anyone else. No two men will agree on what makes a person successful, because success is relative to the individual. While success is relative, we do know that success involves succeeding at a given task. It is also important not to look at what others have done, but concentrate on what you are doing. You should have your own vision. You must learn to have your own measure of success.

It's ok to succeed and it's ok to fail,(if you don't repeat mistakes). Sometimes too much emphasis is put on succeeding, especially for people who hold leadership position. The responsibility is often intense, that creativity is stifled due to fear of failure.

Sometimes the biggest threat to your future success is your current success.

How do you define success?

What have your failures taught you?

What plans do you have to make your future successes more rewarding and fulfilling?

How can your accomplishments be enjoyed and shared with others ?

Time is so precious, money can't buy it, (it's priceless). Time moves on regardless. You cannot manage time, you can only manage priorities. So how we spend our time is very, very important. Do you remember a time when you were sick? You weren't able to do what you wanted to do because the doctor ordered you to rest. Isn't it amazing how all of a sudden what comes to mind is everything you are now unable to do. Too many of us take our time for granted. Regardless of how hectic things get, we should all make time for the really important things in life. Things that give us the most pleasure in life, things that enhance us spiritually.

Life is full of so many wonderful things, too plentiful to mention. You need only spend a little time out of our day to reflect on things that make you happy, or something that puts a smile on your face. A few minutes out of the day, will profit you much, spiritually, emotionally and mentally. In fact you will experience a more enriched and fulfilled day and life.

Here are some things you can do: Listen to music for a minute, Take a walk, Sit in the tub, Play in the mud, Walk in the rain, Walk in the sunshine, Play in the snow, Walk in the sand, Smell flowers, Pray, Watch an ant colony and see how they work together, Play, Feel the breeze on your face, Look at the clouds, Look at the stars, Listen to a friend, Help somebody, Hug somebody, Forgive someone, Tell someone you love them, Forgive yourself.

It's the little things that are important and that make the difference.

The smallest gesture is worth more than the biggest intention.

What things do you like to do?
(Make these things a priority)

How can you take more time for you!

There are two free things that anyone can give children . . . they are love and praise. There are lots of ways to praise children, and express your love for them. These are just a few.

Cool ♥ Wow ♥ You Are Food For My Soul ♥ Way To Go ♥ Super ♥ You're Special ♥ Outstanding ♥ Excellent ♥ Great ♥ I Love You More Than... ♥ Good ♥ Neat ♥ Well Done ♥ Remarkable ♥ I Knew You Could Do It ♥ I'm Proud Of You ♥ Fantastic ♥ Supersta ♥ Nice Work ♥ Looking Good ♥ You're Fantastic ♥ You're On Target ♥ You're On Your Way ♥ You're Right On Top Of It ♥ Bravo ♥ Hurray For You ♥ Beautiful ♥ Now You're Flying ♥ You're Catching On ♥ Now You've Got It ♥ You're Incredible ♥ You're On Your Way ♥ How Nice ♥ How Smart ♥ Good Job ♥ That's Incredible ♥ Hot Dog Dynamite ♥ You're Beautiful ♥ You're Unique ♥ Nothing Can Stop You ♥ Now Good For You ♥ I Like You ♥ You're A Winner ♥ Remarkable Job ♥ Beautiful Work ♥ Spectacular ♥ You're The Best ♥ You're A Darling ♥ You're Precious ♥ Great Discovery ♥ You've Discovered The Secret ♥ You Figured It Out ♥ Fantastic Job ♥ Hip, Hip Hurray ♥ Magnificent ♥ Marvelous ♥ Terrific ♥ You're Important ♥ Phenomenal ♥ You're My Hero ♥ Great ♥ Success ♥ Good Achievement ♥ Exceptional ♥ Astonishing ♥ Amazing ♥ I Admire You ♥ Sensational ♥ Super Work ♥ Super Job ♥ Creative Job ♥ Fantastic Job ♥ Exceptional Performance

You're A Real Trooper ♥ You Are Responsible ♥ You Learned It Right ♥ You Are Amazing ♥ I Admire You ♥ Great Imagination ♥ Sensational ♥ You Learned It Right ♥ What A Good Listener ♥ You Are Exciting ♥ You Tried Hard ♥ Super Worker ♥ Super Job ♥ Creative Job ♥ You Are Responsible ♥ You're Growing Up ♥ You Make Me Laugh ♥ You Tried Hard ♥ Beautiful Sharing ♥ You Care ♥ Outstanding ♥ Perfect Performance ♥ You've Got A Friend ♥ You Brighten My Day ♥ I Trust You You ♥ Mean The World To Me ♥ I Respect You ♥ That's Correct ♥ You're Perfect ♥ You Belong ♥ I Respect You ♥ You're A Treasure ♥ Awesome ♥ You're A Joy ♥ You Are Responsible ♥ Exceptional ♥ I Love You ♥ Fantastic Performance ♥ Fantastic Job ♥ You're A Real Trooper ♥ A Big Hug ♥ A Big Kiss ♥ Well Done!

Praise children and watch them grow into wonderful self motivated, confident adults.

CONNECT

I have found reading one of the most powerful sources for obtaining knowledge, enlightenment and comfort. Until we all become internet friendly (and even after!), there's nothing like a good book. I thought I would share with you some of my favorite books. They are listed in no particular order, but for your convenience, I have used a few words to describe the general essence of each.

Succeeding Against The Odds - by John H. Johnson - The struggles and obstacles faced in entrepreneaurship, by one of today's most successful businessmen.

Live Your Dreams by Les Brown - The path to success, by one of America's greatest speakers.

Uncommon Genius by Denise Shekerjian - A great perspective on the definition of a genius and who one is.

Fully Human by Linda Olds - The importance of integrating both genders.

Ol' The Places You Will Go by Dr.Seuss - The is about believing in yourself and moving on with life.

Alexander Complex by Michael Meyer - How six individuals changed our lives.

As A Man Thinketh by James Allen - The importance of how and what you think, and the effect it has on your life.

Laughing In The Park by Patrice Gaines - Overcoming life's obstacles and moving on to greatness.

Sages And Dreamers by Elie Wiesel - Great historical stories of portraits and legends.

You Can Make It Happen by Steadman Graham - A motivational book with actual guidelines.

In Search Of Holiness by Jerry Bridges Striving to be the best person you can be.

Chicken Sundays by Patricia Polacco - About love, differences, trust and courage. A short read but a good book.

Back To The Family by - About different family types, their composition and their experiences.

The Bible - The greatest stories ever told, with particular emphasis on love, courage, strength, determination, faith and inspiration.

EXPERIENCE

recommended reading

What books would you recommend for reading?

The artwork featured in this book is taken from a collection entitled "Requiem from Distant Lands" , a national museum tribute to the late Claude Monet by the renowned artist Samuel Akainyah. For further information concerning any of the artwork featured herein, Mr. Akainyah can be contacted at The Akainyah Gallery, 357 West Erie, Chicago, Illinois 60611. Telephone 312-654-0333

FORTH COMING BOOKS FROM THE AUTHOR, ABE THOMPSON

"You're a millionaire . . . But Somebody Else Has Your Money"

and

"RELATIONSHIPS - Everything You Need To Know About Developing And Maintaining Good Relationships"

For more information on either of the aforementioned books please visit the website:

www.thoughtsjournalbook.com